Project 2025 Playbook:
Decoding the Right's Master Plan for American Democracy"

Dr. Evelyn Thornridge

DEDICATION

This book is dedicated to the vigilant citizens and steadfast defenders of democracy who tirelessly work to understand, analyze, and engage with the political forces shaping our nation's future.

To those who believe in the power of informed debate and critical thinking, who recognize that the strength of our republic lies in its ability to evolve while preserving its core values.

To the journalists, researchers, activists, and everyday Americans who refuse to take our democratic institutions for granted and who strive to hold power to account, regardless of political affiliation.

And to future generations, who will inherit the consequences of the decisions we make today. May this exploration of Project 2025 contribute to a more nuanced understanding of the challenges and choices facing our democracy.

In the words of Thomas Jefferson, "Eternal vigilance is the price of liberty." May this book serve as a tool for that vigilance.

Contents

Chapitrs

DEDICATION 3

INTRODUCTION 5

The Origins of Project 2025 8

Christian Nationalism and the New Right 13

Dismantling the Administrative State 17

Immigration and Border Security 23

Education Reform and School Choice 29

Abortion and Reproductive Rights 34

LGBTQ Rights and Gender Issues 40

Environmental 46

Deregulation 46

The Unitary Executive Theory 53

Implications for American Democracy 59

Conclusion 64

INTRODUCTION

In the wake of Donald Trump's presidency, a coalition of conservative think tanks and political operatives began crafting an ambitious plan to reshape the federal government and American society. Known as Project 2025, this far-reaching initiative aims to provide a comprehensive blueprint for the next Republican administration to swiftly implement a radical conservative agenda across all areas of policy and governance.

At its core, Project 2025 represents a concerted effort by the American right to consolidate power, roll back progressive gains of recent decades, and fundamentally alter the relationship between citizens and the state. Its proponents envision a future defined by Christian nationalism, limited government, traditionalist social values, and unrestricted free-market capitalism.

This book examines the key components and goals of Project 2025, exploring its origins, ideological underpinnings, and potential consequences for American democracy and society. Drawing on extensive research and analysis, we will dissect the major policy proposals put forth in the project's 920-page "Mandate for Leadership" document published by the Heritage Foundation in April 2023.

From immigration and education to environmental regulation and civil rights, Project 2025 outlines a comprehensive conservative vision for reshaping virtually every aspect of the federal government and American life. Its backers see it as a roadmap for saving the country from what they view as the excesses of liberalism and progressivism. Critics warn it represents a blueprint for dismantling democratic norms and institutions in favor of right-wing authoritarianism.

As the United States approaches another pivotal presidential election in 2024, understanding the aims and implications of Project 2025 is crucial for all Americans, regardless of political affiliation. This initiative provides a stark vision of the country's potential future under renewed conservative governance - one that would have profound and far-reaching impacts on the lives of every citizen.

In the chapters that follow, we will examine the key pillars of Project 2025, exploring its plans for reshaping the federal bureaucracy, overhauling social policies, transforming the education system, restricting immigration, rolling back environmental protections, and centralizing power in the executive branch. We will also analyze the broader ideological goals underpinning these proposals and assess their potential consequences for American democracy, civil liberties, and social cohesion.

By thoroughly dissecting the aims and methods of Project 2025, this book seeks to foster informed public debate about the direction of the country and the competing visions for America's future. Whether one views the initiative as a necessary course correction or a dangerous assault on democratic norms, its far-reaching agenda demands serious scrutiny and discussion as the nation approaches another consequential election.

The story of Project 2025 is, in many ways, the story of the modern American conservative movement - its key players, driving ideologies, and ultimate aspirations for reshaping society. Understanding this ambitious blueprint is essential for comprehending the goals and strategies of the Republican Party and its allies as they seek to chart a new course for the nation.

As we delve into the details of Project 2025 in the coming chapters, readers will gain crucial insight into the potential shape of American governance and society in the years to come. The stakes could not be higher, as this initiative represents nothing less than a roadmap for fundamentally transforming the country according to a distinct ideological vision. Let us begin our exploration of this controversial and consequential plan for America's future.

The Origins of Project 2025

In April 2022, the Heritage Foundation - one of the most influential conservative think tanks in the United States - launched an ambitious initiative called Project 2025. Billed as a comprehensive plan to "restore America," the project brought together a coalition of right-wing organizations, activists, and policy experts to develop a detailed blueprint for conservative governance.

The timing was not coincidental. With the 2024 presidential election on the horizon, Project 2025 was conceived as a ready-made agenda for the next Republican administration. Its architects envisioned a scenario where a conservative president would enter office armed with a fully-formed plan to swiftly reshape the federal government and implement far-reaching policy changes across all domains.

At the helm of Project 2025 was Kevin Roberts, president of the Heritage Foundation and a rising star in conservative policy circles. Under Roberts' leadership, Heritage convened a vast network of right-wing think tanks, advocacy groups, and academic institutions to contribute to the initiative. The project's advisory board eventually grew to include over 100 organizations, representing a veritable who's who of the American conservative movement.

Among the groups involved were longtime conservative powerhouses like the Claremont Institute, the Alliance Defending Freedom, and the American Enterprise Institute. They were joined by newer players on the right such as the Center for Renewing America and the America First Policy Institute - organizations closely aligned with former President Donald Trump and his political movement.

This broad coalition spent months developing detailed policy proposals and strategies for implementing a conservative agenda across all areas of the federal government. Their work culminated in April 2023 with the release of a massive 920-page report titled "Mandate for Leadership: The Conservative Promise to America."

This voluminous document served as the centerpiece of Project 2025, outlining a comprehensive conservative vision for governance. Department by department, agency by agency, it laid out specific plans for reshaping the executive branch and federal bureaucracy to align with right-wing priorities and ideology.

The scope and ambition of the report were staggering. It touched on virtually every aspect of federal policy, from national security and immigration to education, healthcare, and environmental regulation. No area of government was left untouched, as the authors sought to provide a complete roadmap for conservative reform.

In his forward to the report, Kevin Roberts framed Project 2025 as nothing less than a promise to save America from what he described as the failures of the political and cultural elite. He painted a dire picture of a nation beset by inflation, drug addiction, and moral decay - ills he attributed to the influence of progressivism and "woke" ideology.

"Our political class has been discredited by wholesale dishonesty and corruption," Roberts wrote. "Look at America under the ruling and cultural elite today: inflation is ravaging family budgets, drug overdose deaths continue to escalate, and children suffer the toxic normalization of transgenderism."

This stark framing set the tone for the entire Project 2025 initiative. Its architects saw themselves as mounting a crusade to rescue the country from the grip of liberal elites and restore traditional American values. To achieve this, they were prepared to pursue sweeping changes across all levels of government and society.

The release of the "Mandate for Leadership" report marked a significant moment in the evolution of the conservative movement. Never before had such a comprehensive and detailed plan for right-wing governance been assembled. Project 2025 represented the culmination of decades of conservative policy development, packaged into an actionable blueprint for reshaping America.

As news of Project 2025 began to spread, it elicited strong reactions across the political spectrum. Conservatives hailed it as a visionary roadmap for restoring the country to its proper path. Liberals and progressives decried it as a dangerous assault on democratic norms and civil liberties.

What was clear to all observers, however, was that Project 2025 represented a watershed moment in American politics. It signaled the emergence of a newly emboldened and unapologetic conservative movement, one that was no longer content to simply resist progressive change but sought to actively roll back decades of liberal policies and remake society in its own image.

As we will explore in the coming chapters, the agenda laid out in Project 2025 touches on virtually every aspect of American life. From transforming the education system to reshaping immigration policy, from rolling back environmental protections to restricting reproductive rights, its proposals would have profound implications for all citizens.

Understanding the origins and aims of Project 2025 is crucial for comprehending the current state of American conservatism and the potential future of governance under Republican leadership. In the chapters that follow, we will delve deeper into the key pillars of this ambitious plan, examining its specific proposals and their potential consequences for the nation.

In his forward to the report, Kevin Roberts framed Project 2025 as nothing less than a promise to save America from what he described as the failures of the political and cultural elite. He painted a dire picture of a nation beset by inflation, drug addiction, and moral decay - ills he attributed to the influence of progressivism and "woke" ideology.

"Our political class has been discredited by wholesale dishonesty and corruption," Roberts wrote. "Look at America under the ruling and cultural elite today: inflation is ravaging family budgets, drug overdose deaths continue to escalate, and children suffer the toxic normalization of transgenderism."

This stark framing set the tone for the entire Project 2025 initiative. Its architects saw themselves as mounting a crusade to rescue the country from the grip of liberal elites and restore traditional American values. To achieve this, they were prepared to pursue sweeping changes across all levels of government and society.

The release of the "Mandate for Leadership" report marked a significant moment in the evolution of the conservative movement. Never before had such a comprehensive and detailed plan for right-wing governance been assembled. Project 2025 represented the culmination of decades of conservative policy development, packaged into an actionable blueprint for reshaping America.

Christian Nationalism and the New Right

At the heart of Project 2025 lies a vision of America deeply rooted in Christian nationalist ideology. This worldview, which has gained increasing prominence within the conservative movement in recent years, seeks to redefine the United States as an explicitly Christian nation whose laws and institutions should be based on a particular interpretation of biblical principles.

The influence of Christian nationalism is evident throughout the "Mandate for Leadership" document that forms the core of Project 2025. Its authors repeatedly invoke religious language and concepts, framing their policy proposals not just as political choices but as moral imperatives grounded in Christian teaching.

This merging of religious ideology with conservative politics represents a significant shift in the American right. While appeals to faith and traditional values have long been a staple of Republican rhetoric, Project 2025 goes further in explicitly calling for the reshaping of government and society along Christian nationalist lines.

Kevin Roberts, the Heritage Foundation president spearheading Project 2025, made this religious framing clear in his introduction to the initiative. He declared that "the very moral foundations of our society are in peril" and positioned the project as a crusade to restore America's supposed Christian character.

This emphasis on Christian nationalism is reflected in many of the specific policy proposals put forth in Project 2025. For instance, the initiative calls for:

- - Redefining religious liberty to allow for greater discrimination against LGBTQ individuals and others on the basis of religious beliefs
- - Promoting prayer and Bible study in public schools
- - Restricting access to abortion and contraception based on religious objections
- - Prioritizing traditional "family values" in all areas of social policy
- - Reshaping foreign policy to more explicitly favor Christian nations and interests

These proposals represent a concerted effort to elevate a particular interpretation of Christianity to a position of legal and cultural dominance within American society. Critics warn that such moves threaten the constitutional separation of church and state and risk marginalizing religious minorities and non-believers.

Proponents of Christian nationalism, however, reject the notion of a secular state entirely. They argue that America was founded as a Christian nation and that a return to these purported roots is necessary to address what they see as moral and social decay.

This worldview is perhaps most clearly articulated by Jack Posobiec, a prominent right-wing media figure and supporter of Project 2025. Speaking at the 2024 Conservative Political Action Conference, Posobiec declared the initiative's goal was to "destroy democracy" and replace it with a system of governance based on Christian principles.

While such rhetoric may seem extreme, it reflects a strain of thought that has become increasingly influential within the conservative movement. Project 2025 represents an attempt to translate this Christian nationalist ideology into concrete policy proposals and governance strategies.

The implications of this shift are far-reaching. If implemented, the agenda laid out in Project 2025 would fundamentally alter the relationship between religion and government in the United States. It would prioritize a particular interpretation of Christianity in law and policy, potentially marginalizing other faith traditions and non-religious Americans.

Moreover, the Christian nationalist framework underpinning Project 2025 shapes its approach to a wide range of issues beyond explicitly religious matters. Its influence can be seen in proposals related to education, healthcare, environmental policy, and foreign affairs.

For instance, the initiative's approach to climate change is heavily influenced by a religious worldview that rejects mainstream scientific consensus. Similarly, its stance on issues like gender and sexuality is rooted in conservative Christian teachings rather than contemporary medical or psychological understanding.

This merging of religious ideology with public policy represents a significant challenge to the traditional liberal democratic order. It raises fundamental questions about the nature of religious liberty, the role of faith in governance, and the rights of religious minorities in a diverse society.

As we examine the specific proposals put forth in Project 2025 in subsequent chapters, it will be crucial to consider how this Christian nationalist framework shapes and informs the initiative's overall vision for America. Understanding this ideological underpinning is essential for grasping the full implications of the project's ambitious agenda.

The rise of Christian nationalism as a driving force in conservative politics represents a significant shift in the American political landscape. Project 2025 stands as perhaps the most comprehensive attempt yet to translate this worldview into a concrete plan for governance.

Whether one views this development as a necessary course correction or a dangerous departure from democratic norms, its potential impact on American society cannot be overstated. The Christian nationalist vision at the heart of Project 2025 would, if implemented, reshape virtually every aspect of life in the United States.

As we continue our exploration of this far-reaching initiative, we must grapple with the profound questions it raises about the future of American democracy, the role of religion in public life, and the very nature of the nation itself. The answers to these questions will play a crucial role in determining the course of the country in the years to come.

Dismantling the Administrative State

One of the central goals of Project 2025 is the dramatic reduction and restructuring of the federal bureaucracy. This objective, often framed as "dismantling the administrative state," represents a long-standing conservative ambition to roll back the expansion of government that has occurred since the New Deal era.

The "Mandate for Leadership" document outlines a comprehensive strategy for shrinking the size and scope of the federal government across virtually all domains. This approach is rooted in a deeply held conservative belief that an overgrown bureaucracy stifles economic growth, infringes on individual liberty, and undermines the constitutional separation of powers.

At the heart of this effort is a plan to significantly reduce the federal workforce. Project 2025 calls for the elimination of tens of thousands of government jobs, targeting what its authors describe as "unnecessary" or "redundant" positions across various agencies and departments.

This proposed culling of the federal workforce would be achieved through a combination of hiring freezes, early retirement incentives, and outright terminations. The initiative also calls for making it easier to fire government employees by stripping away long-standing civil service protections.

A key mechanism for this proposed overhaul is the resurrection of "Schedule F," an executive order briefly implemented during the Trump administration. This order would reclassify a significant portion of the federal workforce, removing their employment protections and making them more easily replaceable.

Critics warn that such moves could lead to a politicization of the civil service, allowing incoming administrations to purge career officials and replace them with ideological allies. Proponents argue it is necessary to ensure the bureaucracy aligns with the elected president's agenda.

Beyond reducing the size of the workforce, Project 2025 also calls for a fundamental restructuring of many federal agencies and departments. This includes proposals to:

- - Eliminate entire cabinet-level departments, such as the Department of Education and the Department of Energy
- - Break up larger agencies into smaller, more focused entities
- - Consolidate overlapping functions across different parts of the government
- - Devolve many federal responsibilities to state and local governments

The rationale behind these proposed changes is to create a leaner, more efficient federal government that exercises less control over various aspects of American life. However, critics argue that such dramatic cuts could severely impair the government's ability to carry out essential functions and respond to crises.

One of the most controversial aspects of this plan to dismantle the administrative state is its approach to regulatory agencies. Project 2025 calls for significantly curtailing the power of bodies like the Environmental Protection Agency, the Food and Drug Administration, and the Securities and Exchange Commission.

The initiative proposes achieving this through a combination of budget cuts, staffing reductions, and new restrictions on agencies' ability to create and enforce regulations. This would represent a dramatic shift in how the federal government oversees various industries and protects public health and safety.

Proponents argue that excessive regulation stifles economic growth and innovation. They contend that rolling back the regulatory state will unleash American entrepreneurship and prosperity. Critics warn that such moves could lead to increased pollution, financial instability, and threats to public health and consumer safety.

The "Mandate for Leadership" also outlines plans to bring independent agencies more directly under presidential control. This includes proposals to give the president greater power to hire and fire the heads of agencies like the Federal Reserve, the Federal Communications Commission, and the National Labor Relations Board.

Such changes would represent a significant shift in how these agencies operate, potentially making them more susceptible to political influence. Supporters argue this is necessary to ensure accountability, while critics warn it could undermine the agencies' independence and expertise.

This power, which was curtailed by Congress in the 1970s following abuses by the Nixon administration, would give the executive branch significant leverage over spending priorities. Critics argue this could upset the constitutional balance of powers, while proponents see it as a necessary tool for reining in government spending.

Project 2025 also proposes sweeping changes to how federal regulations are created and implemented. This includes calls for:

- - Requiring congressional approval for major new regulations
- - Instituting automatic sunset provisions for existing regulations
- - Mandating cost-benefit analyses for all new rules
- - Expanding opportunities for affected industries to challenge regulations in court

Collectively, these changes would make it significantly more difficult for federal agencies to create and enforce new rules. Supporters argue this is necessary to prevent regulatory overreach, while critics warn it could lead to a dangerous rollback of important protections.

The initiative's plans for dismantling the administrative state extend beyond just the federal level. Project 2025 also outlines strategies for encouraging states to reduce their own bureaucracies and regulatory apparatuses. This includes proposals for new federal incentives to reward states that cut regulations and shrink their governments.

Underlying all of these proposals is a fundamental reimagining of the role of government in American society. The architects of Project 2025 envision a dramatically reduced federal presence in many areas of life, with greater power devolved to states, localities, and the private sector.

This vision represents a sharp departure from the expansive view of government that has dominated American politics since the New Deal era. It harks back to a more limited conception of federal power that prevailed in the 19th century, before the rise of the modern regulatory state.

Proponents argue that this scaling back of government is necessary to restore individual liberty, promote economic dynamism, and return to a more faithful interpretation of the Constitution. They contend that decades of bureaucratic expansion have stifled American innovation and eroded democratic accountability.

Critics, however, warn that such a dramatic rollback of the federal government could have severe consequences. They argue that many of the agencies and regulations targeted by Project 2025 play crucial roles in protecting public health, ensuring workplace safety, safeguarding the environment, and maintaining economic stability.

Moreover, opponents contend that the initiative's plans for reshaping the federal workforce could lead to a dangerous politicization of the civil service. They warn that making it easier to fire career officials and replace them with political appointees could undermine the expertise and continuity necessary for effective governance.

The debate over the proper size and scope of government has been a defining feature of American politics for generations. Project 2025 represents perhaps the most ambitious and comprehensive plan yet put forward for dramatically shrinking and reshaping the federal bureaucracy.

If implemented, the changes proposed in the "Mandate for Leadership" would fundamentally alter the relationship between citizens and their government. They would roll back decades of expansions in federal authority and responsibility, potentially transforming virtually every aspect of how the government interacts with society.

As we continue our examination of Project 2025, it will be crucial to consider the full implications of this proposed dismantling of the administrative state. The consequences of such sweeping changes would likely be felt in every corner of American life, from the air we breathe and the food we eat to the safety of our workplaces and the stability of our financial system.

Whether one views these proposals as a necessary corrective to bureaucratic overreach or a dangerous assault on essential protections, their potential impact cannot be overstated. The vision of a radically reduced federal government outlined in Project 2025 represents nothing less than a fundamental reimagining of the American state and its role in society.

Immigration and Border Security

One of the most contentious and far-reaching aspects of Project 2025 is its approach to immigration and border security. The initiative outlines a series of dramatic proposals aimed at significantly reducing both legal and illegal immigration to the United States, representing perhaps the most restrictionist vision of American immigration policy put forward in modern times.

At the heart of these proposals is a fundamental reimagining of America's relationship with immigration. Where the United States has long viewed itself as a nation of immigrants, Project 2025 envisions a much more closed and selective approach to allowing new arrivals into the country.

The "Mandate for Leadership" document calls for a range of measures to drastically curtail immigration, including:

- - Constructing a complete physical barrier along the entire U.S.-Mexico border
- - Implementing a "zero tolerance" policy for illegal border crossings, with mandatory criminal prosecution for all violators
- - Dramatically reducing the number of legal immigrants admitted to the country each year
- - Eliminating the diversity visa lottery program
- - Ending family-based "chain migration" beyond spouses and minor children

- Imposing new restrictions on asylum claims and refugee admissions
- Mandating the use of E-Verify for all employers to check workers' immigration status

These proposals go far beyond simply enhancing border security or cracking down on illegal immigration. They represent a fundamental shift in how America approaches the very concept of immigration, moving away from the nation's traditional role as a beacon for those seeking a better life.

One of the most controversial aspects of Project 2025's immigration plan is its approach to those already in the country illegally. The initiative calls for a massive increase in deportations, proposing to remove millions of undocumented immigrants over a short period.

To achieve this, the plan outlines strategies for ramping up interior enforcement, including:

- - Hiring thousands of new Immigration and Customs Enforcement (ICE) agents
- - Expanding detention capacity to hold more immigrants awaiting deportation
- - Cutting federal funding to "sanctuary cities" that limit cooperation with immigration authorities
- - Implementing a national biometric entry-exit system to track visa overstays
- - Expanding the use of expedited removal procedures to quickly deport recent arrivals

Critics warn that such aggressive enforcement measures could lead to family separations, rights violations, and the creation of a climate of fear in immigrant communities. Proponents argue they are necessary to restore the rule of law and protect American workers and taxpayers.

Project 2025 also proposes significant changes to legal immigration programs. The initiative calls for transitioning to a "merit-based" system that would prioritize highly skilled immigrants over family reunification. This would represent a dramatic departure from current U.S. immigration policy, which has long emphasized family ties.

The plan also seeks to reduce overall levels of legal immigration by up to 50%, arguing that current numbers are too high and harm American workers. This would be achieved through a combination of lower annual caps, stricter eligibility criteria, and the elimination of certain visa categories.

One particularly controversial proposal calls for ending birthright citizenship for children born in the U.S. to non-citizen parents. This would require either a constitutional amendment or a reinterpretation of the 14th Amendment, and would represent a seismic shift in how America defines citizenship.

Project 2025 also outlines plans for reshaping the agencies responsible for immigration enforcement and administration. This includes proposals to:

- - Break up the Department of Homeland Security, spinning off immigration functions into a new agency
- - Strip the Department of Justice of its authority over immigration courts, creating a new independent tribunal system
- - Expand the authority of state and local law enforcement to enforce federal immigration laws

enforced in the United States. Critics argue they could lead to a more politicized and less accountable system, while supporters contend they are necessary for more effective enforcement.

The initiative's approach to refugees and asylum seekers has drawn particular criticism from human rights advocates. Project 2025 calls for dramatically reducing the number of refugees admitted to the U.S. each year and imposing new restrictions on asylum claims.

Proposed measures include:

- - Requiring asylum seekers to apply from outside the U.S. or at designated points of entry
- - Implementing a "safe third country" agreement with Mexico to return Central American asylum seekers
- - Expanding the use of detention for asylum applicants while their cases are pending
- - Narrowing the criteria for granting asylum, particularly for claims based on gang or domestic violence

Supporters argue these changes are necessary to prevent abuse of the asylum system and ensure that only those with legitimate claims receive protection. Critics contend they would effectively shut the door on many vulnerable individuals fleeing persecution and violence.

The immigration proposals outlined in Project 2025 reflect a broader ideological shift within the conservative movement towards a more restrictionist and nationalist approach to border policy. This represents a departure from the more pro-immigration stance traditionally held by many business-oriented Republicans.

This new approach is rooted in concerns about the cultural and demographic changes brought about by high levels of immigration. Many of the initiative's backers argue that current immigration patterns are altering the character of American society in ways they view as detrimental.

Critics, however, warn that such a dramatic reduction in immigration could have severe economic consequences. They point to studies showing that immigrants play a crucial role in many sectors of the U.S. economy and argue that sharp cuts to immigration could lead to labor shortages and reduced economic growth.

Moreover, opponents contend that the harsh enforcement measures proposed in Project 2025 could lead to widespread civil rights violations and damage America's image as a welcoming nation. They argue that such an approach runs counter to core American values and traditions.

The debate over immigration policy has long been one of the most contentious in American politics. Project 2025's proposals represent perhaps the most comprehensive attempt yet to reshape the nation's approach to this complex issue.

If implemented, the changes outlined in the "Mandate for Leadership" would fundamentally alter America's relationship with immigration and its role as a destination for those seeking a better life. The consequences of such a shift would be felt not just at the border, but throughout American society and economy.

As we continue our examination of Project 2025, it will be crucial to consider the full implications of these proposed changes to immigration policy. The vision put forward by the initiative's architects would reshape not just how America manages its borders, but how it defines itself as a nation.

Whether one views these proposals as a necessary corrective to decades of lax enforcement or a betrayal of core American values, their potential impact cannot be overstated. The immigration plan outlined in Project 2025 represents nothing less than a fundamental reimagining of America's identity as a nation of immigrants.

Education Reform and School Choice

Education reform stands as one of the central pillars of Project 2025, with the initiative outlining a sweeping vision for reshaping America's public education system. At the heart of this plan is a push for expanded school choice and a dramatic reduction in federal involvement in education policy.

The "Mandate for Leadership" document calls for a fundamental reimagining of the federal government's role in education, proposing to:

- Eliminate the Department of Education as a cabinet-level agency
- Block grant all federal education funding to states with minimal strings attached
- Expand school choice programs, including vouchers and charter schools
- Roll back federal civil rights enforcement in education
- Promote traditional curriculum and teaching methods

These proposals represent a dramatic departure from decades of federal education policy, which has seen an expanding role for Washington in shaping standards, enforcing equity, and providing funding for public schools.

Proponents argue that these changes are necessary to improve educational outcomes, empower parents, and respect local control over schooling. Critics warn they could exacerbate educational inequalities and undermine crucial protections for vulnerable students.

One of the most significant aspects of Project 2025's education plan is its push for expanded school choice. The initiative calls for a massive increase in federal support for voucher programs, which provide public funds for students to attend private or religious schools.

Specifically, the plan proposes:

- - Creating a federal tax credit scholarship program to fund private school tuition
- - Expanding the use of 529 savings accounts to cover K-12 private school expenses
- - Providing vouchers for students in underperforming public schools to attend private institutions
- - Increasing federal support for charter schools and other alternative education models

Supporters argue that these measures would give parents more control over their children's education and foster competition that improves all schools. Critics contend that voucher programs drain resources from public schools and can exacerbate segregation.

Project 2025 also outlines plans for dramatically reducing the federal government's role in setting education standards and enforcing civil rights in schools. This includes proposals to:

- - Repeal the Every Student Succeeds Act and its testing requirements
- - End federal oversight of state accountability systems
- - Scale back the Department of Education's Office for Civil Rights
- - Prohibit federal funding for schools that teach "critical race theory" or "gender ideology"

These moves would represent a significant rollback of federal involvement in education policy, potentially leading to greater variation in standards and practices across states and districts. Proponents argue this is necessary to restore local control, while critics warn it could lead to a reduction in educational quality and equity.

Another key aspect of Project 2025's education plan is its emphasis on promoting traditional curriculum and teaching methods. The initiative calls for:

- - Encouraging states to adopt phonics-based reading instruction
- - Promoting the teaching of "classical" literature and history
- - Emphasizing STEM education and vocational training
- - Discouraging the use of "progressive" teaching methods like social-emotional learning

These proposals reflect a broader conservative critique of what they see as left-leaning bias in public education. Critics argue that such prescriptive approaches to curriculum infringe on academic freedom and local control.

Project 2025 also outlines plans for reshaping higher education policy. This includes proposals to:

- - End federal student loan programs and transition to a private lending system
- - Eliminate affirmative action in college admissions
- - Restrict federal funding for universities that are deemed to suppress free speech
- - Promote alternatives to traditional four-year degrees, such as vocational programs

These changes would represent a significant shift in how higher education is funded and regulated in the United States. Proponents argue they are necessary to address rising costs and ideological bias on campuses, while critics warn they could reduce access to higher education and stifle academic freedom.

Underlying all of these proposals is a fundamental reimagining of the purpose and structure of American education. The architects of Project 2025 envision a system with less federal oversight, more parental choice, and a greater emphasis on traditional academic content and vocational skills.

This vision represents a sharp departure from the trends that have dominated education policy in recent decades. It pushes back against efforts to use schools as a tool for promoting equity and social justice, instead emphasizing individual choice and traditional academic rigor.

Proponents argue that this approach will lead to better educational outcomes and more satisfied parents and students. They contend that the current system, with its emphasis on standardized testing and federal oversight, has failed to improve results despite massive increases in spending.

Critics, however, warn that the changes proposed in Project 2025 could exacerbate educational inequalities and roll back important protections for vulnerable students. They argue that strong federal oversight is necessary to ensure that all children, regardless of background, have access to quality education.

Moreover, opponents contend that many of the initiative's proposals, particularly around curriculum and teaching methods, represent an inappropriate intrusion of partisan politics into education. They warn that attempts to dictate what can and cannot be taught in schools threaten academic freedom and critical thinking.

The debate over education policy has long been one of the most contentious in American politics, touching on fundamental questions about the role of government, individual rights, and the purpose of schooling. Project 2025 represents perhaps the most comprehensive conservative vision yet put forward for reshaping the nation's approach to education.

If implemented, the changes outlined in the "Mandate for Leadership" would fundamentally alter how education is delivered, funded, and regulated in the United States. The consequences of such a shift would be felt not just in classrooms, but throughout American society and economy.

As we continue our examination of Project 2025, it will be crucial to consider the full implications of these proposed changes to education policy. The vision put forward by the initiative's architects would reshape not just how America educates its children, but how it prepares its citizens for the challenges of the 21st century.

Whether one views these proposals as a necessary corrective to decades of failed policies or a dangerous assault on public education, their potential impact cannot be overstated. The education plan outlined in Project 2025 represents nothing less than a fundamental reimagining of one of society's most crucial institutions.

Abortion and Reproductive Rights

Few issues in Project 2025 are as contentious or far-reaching as its approach to abortion and reproductive rights. The initiative outlines an aggressive strategy for restricting access to abortion and contraception, representing perhaps the most comprehensive pro-life policy agenda ever put forward at the federal level.

At the heart of these proposals is a fundamental redefinition of when life begins and what rights should be accorded to fetuses. Project 2025 calls for enshrining in law the principle that human life begins at conception, with all the legal and policy implications that would entail.

Specifically, the "Mandate for Leadership" document proposes:

- - Passing a federal "heartbeat bill" banning abortions after fetal cardiac activity is detected
- - Eliminating all federal funding for organizations that provide or refer for abortions
- - Appointing pro-life judges to federal courts, including the Supreme Court
- - Rescinding FDA approval for abortion drugs like mifepristone
- - Implementing new restrictions on fetal tissue research
- - Expanding "conscience protections" for healthcare workers who object to providing abortion or contraception

These proposals go far beyond simply limiting access to abortion. They represent a fundamental reimagining of reproductive rights in America, with potentially far-reaching consequences for women's healthcare, medical research, and personal autonomy.

One of the most controversial aspects of Project 2025's reproductive rights agenda is its approach to contraception. While not calling for an outright ban, the initiative proposes several measures that could significantly restrict access to birth control, including:

- - Eliminating the Affordable Care Act's contraceptive coverage mandate
- - Restricting federal Title X family planning funds to organizations that do not provide abortions
- - Promoting "natural family planning" methods over hormonal contraceptives
- - Expanding the ability of employers to opt out of providing contraceptive coverage based on religious or moral objections

Critics warn that such measures could lead to an increase in unintended pregnancies and, paradoxically, more abortions. Proponents argue they are necessary to protect religious liberty and promote a "culture of life."

Project 2025 also outlines plans for reshaping how abortion and reproductive health are discussed and researched in America. This includes proposals to:

- - Mandate that abortion providers offer ultrasounds and information about fetal development
- - Implement new reporting requirements for abortion providers
- - Restrict federal funding for sex education programs that discuss abortion
- - Promote adoption as an alternative to abortion
- - Fund research into the purported negative psychological effects of abortion

These measures reflect a broader conservative strategy of using information and persuasion to discourage abortion, even in cases where it remains legal. Critics argue that such approaches can be coercive and may spread misinformation.

One particularly controversial aspect of Project 2025's reproductive rights agenda is its approach to enforcing abortion restrictions across state lines. The initiative proposes measures to prevent women from traveling to other states to obtain abortions, including:

- - Allowing states to prosecute individuals who help women obtain out-of-state abortions
- - Implementing a federal ban on shipping abortion drugs across state lines
- - Creating a national database to track women who have had abortions

Such proposals raise significant constitutional questions and have been sharply criticized by civil liberties advocates. Proponents argue they are necessary to prevent the circumvention of state-level abortion restrictions.

Project 2025 also outlines plans for reshaping federal agencies involved in reproductive health policy. This includes proposals to:

- - Appoint pro-life leadership to key positions at the Department of Health and Human Services
- - Redirect federal family planning funds towards crisis pregnancy centers
- - Eliminate offices within HHS focused on women's health and reproductive rights
- - Create new divisions focused on "protecting life" and promoting adoption

These structural changes would significantly alter how reproductive health policy is implemented at the federal level. Critics argue they could lead to a politicization of public health, while supporters contend they are necessary to align government policy with pro-life principles.

The initiative's approach to international reproductive health policy has also drawn scrutiny. Project 2025 calls for:

- - Reinstating and expanding the "Mexico City Policy" prohibiting U.S. aid to organizations that provide or promote abortion overseas
- - Withdrawing funding from the United Nations Population Fund
- - Promoting pro-life policies in international forums and aid programs

Such measures would represent a significant shift in U.S. foreign policy on reproductive health issues, potentially impacting millions of women in developing countries.

Underlying all of these proposals is a fundamental reimagining of reproductive rights in America. The architects of Project 2025 envision a society where abortion is not just restricted, but culturally and legally unacceptable in most circumstances.

This vision represents a dramatic departure from the legal and cultural norms that have prevailed since the Roe v. Wade decision in 1973. It pushes back against the idea of reproductive choice as a fundamental right, instead framing abortion as a moral wrong that should be discouraged and restricted by government policy.

Proponents argue that this approach is necessary to protect the rights of unborn children and promote a "culture of life." They contend that decades of legalized abortion have devalued human life and harmed women.

Critics, however, warn that the changes proposed in Project 2025 would represent a dangerous rollback of women's rights and could have severe consequences for public health. They argue that restricting access to abortion and contraception would lead to more unintended pregnancies, unsafe abortions, and negative health outcomes for women.

Moreover, opponents contend that many of the initiative's proposals infringe on personal privacy and bodily autonomy. They warn that attempts to track and prosecute women seeking abortions across state lines represent a troubling expansion of government surveillance and control.

The debate over abortion and reproductive rights has long been one of the most divisive in American politics. Project 2025 represents perhaps the most comprehensive attempt yet to reshape the nation's approach to these issues from a pro-life perspective.

If implemented, the changes outlined in the "Mandate for Leadership" would fundamentally alter how reproductive healthcare is delivered, regulated, and understood in the United States. The consequences of such a shift would be felt not just in doctor's offices and hospitals, but throughout American society.

As we continue our examination of Project 2025, it will be crucial to consider the full implications of these proposed changes to reproductive rights policy. The vision put forward by the initiative's architects would reshape not just how America approaches abortion, but how it conceives of personal autonomy, medical ethics, and the role of government in intimate personal decisions.

Whether one views these proposals as a necessary protection for unborn life or a dangerous assault on women's rights, their potential impact cannot be overstated. The reproductive rights plan outlined in Project 2025 represents nothing less than a fundamental reimagining of one of the most contentious issues in American politics and society.

LGBTQ Rights and Gender Issues

Project 2025's approach to LGBTQ rights and gender issues represents one of its most controversial and far-reaching aspects. The initiative outlines a comprehensive strategy for rolling back many of the legal and social gains made by the LGBTQ community in recent decades, framing these efforts as necessary to protect traditional values and religious liberty.

At the core of these proposals is a fundamental rejection of the concept of gender identity as distinct from biological sex. Project 2025 calls for enshrining in law and policy the principle that sex is immutable and binary, with significant implications for transgender rights and gender-affirming care.

Specifically, the "Mandate for Leadership" document proposes:

- - Defining sex as binary and immutable in all federal laws and regulations
- - Banning gender-affirming care for minors at the federal level
- - Prohibiting transgender individuals from serving in the military
- - Rescinding Obama-era guidance on transgender students' rights in schools
- - Expanding religious exemptions to allow discrimination against LGBTQ individuals
- - Eliminating LGBTQ-inclusive curriculum in schools receiving federal funding

These proposals represent a dramatic departure from the trends of increasing LGBTQ acceptance and rights protection that have characterized recent years. They signal a concerted effort to not just halt, but reverse the progress made on these issues.

One of the most contentious aspects of Project 2025's LGBTQ agenda is its approach to transgender rights. The initiative calls for a series of measures that would significantly restrict the ability of transgender individuals to live according to their gender identity, including:

- - Prohibiting changes to sex markers on federal documents like passports
- - Mandating that federally-funded programs and facilities (including prisons and shelters) segregate by biological sex rather than gender identity
- - Banning coverage of gender-affirming treatments under federal health programs
- - Restricting the ability of transgender athletes to compete in accordance with their gender identity

Critics warn that such measures could lead to increased discrimination, violence, and mental health challenges for transgender individuals. Proponents argue they are necessary to protect women's spaces and maintain clear biological distinctions.

Project 2025 also outlines plans for reshaping how LGBTQ issues are discussed and researched in America. This includes proposals to:

- - Fund research into the purported negative effects of gender transition
- - Promote "ex-gay" or conversion therapy as an option for individuals experiencing same-sex attraction
- - Restrict federal funding for LGBTQ-inclusive sex education programs
- - Mandate that schools inform parents if their children express gender nonconformity

These measures reflect a broader conservative strategy of using information and persuasion to discourage LGBTQ identities and behaviors, even in cases where they remain legal. Critics argue that such approaches can be harmful and may spread misinformation.

One particularly controversial aspect of Project 2025's LGBTQ rights agenda is its approach to religious exemptions. The initiative proposes expanding the ability of individuals, businesses, and organizations to discriminate against LGBTQ people based on religious beliefs. This includes:

- Creating broad religious exemptions to non-discrimination laws
- Allowing faith-based adoption agencies to refuse placement with same-sex couples
- Permitting healthcare providers to refuse treatment to LGBTQ patients
- Protecting the ability of businesses to deny service to LGBTQ customers

Such proposals raise significant civil rights concerns and have been sharply criticized by LGBTQ advocates. Proponents argue they are necessary to protect religious liberty and freedom of conscience.

Project 2025 also outlines plans for reshaping federal agencies involved in civil rights enforcement. This includes proposals to:

- Appoint leadership opposed to LGBTQ rights to key positions at the Department of Justice and Equal Employment Opportunity Commission
- Eliminate LGBTQ-focused offices and initiatives within federal agencies
- Redirect federal civil rights enforcement away from LGBTQ discrimination cases

These structural changes would significantly alter how civil rights laws are interpreted and enforced at the federal level. Critics argue they could lead to a rollback of crucial protections, while supporters contend they are necessary to refocus government priorities.

The initiative's approach to international LGBTQ rights policy has also drawn scrutiny. Project 2025 calls for:

- - Ending U.S. advocacy for LGBTQ rights in international forums
- - Withdrawing from international agreements that recognize LGBTQ rights
- - Redirecting foreign aid away from LGBTQ-focused programs

Such measures would represent a significant shift in U.S. foreign policy on LGBTQ issues, potentially impacting millions of people in countries where these rights are already precarious.

Underlying all of these proposals is a fundamental reimagining of LGBTQ rights and gender identity in America. The architects of Project 2025 envision a society where non-traditional gender identities and sexual orientations are not just unprotected, but actively discouraged through government policy.

This vision represents a dramatic departure from the legal and cultural trends of increasing LGBTQ acceptance that have characterized recent decades. It pushes back against the idea of LGBTQ rights as civil rights, instead framing them as a threat to traditional values and religious liberty.

Proponents argue that this approach is necessary to protect children, preserve traditional family structures, and safeguard religious freedom. They contend that the rapid expansion of LGBTQ rights has gone too far and threatens fundamental social institutions.

Critics, however, warn that the changes proposed in Project 2025 would represent a dangerous rollback of hard-won civil rights protections. They argue that restricting LGBTQ rights and gender-affirming care could lead to increased discrimination, violence, and negative mental health outcomes for LGBTQ individuals, particularly youth.

Moreover, opponents contend that many of the initiative's proposals infringe on personal privacy and individual liberty. They warn that attempts to restrict how people express their gender identity or sexual orientation represent a troubling expansion of government control over intimate personal matters.

The debate over LGBTQ rights and gender issues has become increasingly polarized in American politics. Project 2025 represents perhaps the most comprehensive attempt yet to reshape the nation's approach to these issues from a traditionalist perspective.

If implemented, the changes outlined in the "Mandate for Leadership" would fundamentally alter how LGBTQ rights are understood and protected in the United States. The consequences of such a shift would be felt not just in courtrooms and legislatures, but throughout American society.

As we continue our examination of Project 2025, it will be crucial to consider the full implications of these proposed changes to LGBTQ rights and gender policy. The vision put forward by the initiative's architects would reshape not just how America approaches these issues legally, but how it conceives of gender, sexuality, and personal identity more broadly.

Whether one views these proposals as a necessary protection for traditional values or a dangerous assault on civil rights, their potential impact cannot be overstated. The LGBTQ rights plan outlined in Project 2025 represents nothing less than a fundamental reimagining of one of the most rapidly evolving areas of American law and society.

The tension between advancing LGBTQ rights and protecting religious liberty has become a defining feature of America's culture wars. Project 2025's approach to resolving this tension decisively in favor of religious conservatives would, if implemented, have profound implications for millions of LGBTQ Americans and for the broader fabric of civil rights law in the United States.

As society continues to grapple with changing understandings of gender and sexuality, the vision laid out in Project 2025 stands as a stark counterpoint to recent trends towards greater acceptance and legal protection for LGBTQ individuals. The debate over these proposals is likely to remain at the forefront of American political discourse for years to come.

Environmental Deregulation

Project 2025's approach to environmental policy represents one of its most sweeping and potentially consequential aspects. The initiative outlines a comprehensive strategy for rolling back decades of environmental regulations, framing these efforts as necessary to promote economic growth and energy independence.

At the core of these proposals is a fundamental rejection of the scientific consensus on climate change and a prioritization of fossil fuel development over environmental protection. Project 2025 calls for a dramatic reduction in the federal government's role in environmental regulation, with significant implications for air and water quality, wildlife conservation, and global climate efforts.

Specifically, the "Mandate for Leadership" document proposes:

- - Withdrawing from the Paris Climate Agreement and other international environmental accords
- - Eliminating or significantly weakening the Environmental Protection Agency
- - Repealing the Clean Power Plan and other Obama-era climate regulations
- - Expanding oil, gas, and coal production on federal lands and offshore areas
- - Revoking California's waiver to set stricter vehicle emissions standards
- - Overhauling the Endangered Species Act to reduce protections for wildlife
- - Rolling back fuel efficiency standards for vehicles

These proposals represent a dramatic departure from the environmental policies that have shaped American governance for the past half-century. They signal a concerted effort to not just halt, but reverse many of the environmental protections put in place since the 1970s.

One of the most contentious aspects of Project 2025's environmental agenda is its approach to climate change. The initiative calls for a series of measures that would significantly curtail efforts to reduce greenhouse gas emissions and adapt to a warming planet, including:

- - Prohibiting federal agencies from considering climate change in policymaking
- - Eliminating funding for climate change research and monitoring
- - Rescinding the EPA's authority to regulate greenhouse gases under the Clean Air Act
- - Promoting "climate change skepticism" in federal communications and educational materials
- - Withdrawing support for renewable energy development and research
-

Critics warn that such measures could have catastrophic long-term consequences for the planet and future generations. Proponents argue they are necessary to protect American energy independence and economic competitiveness.

Project 2025 also outlines plans for reshaping how environmental issues are researched and discussed in America. This includes proposals to:

- - Overhaul the peer review process for environmental research to include more industry perspectives
- - Restrict the types of scientific studies that can be used to justify environmental regulations

- - Promote "balance" in media coverage of environmental issues by amplifying skeptical voices
- - Revise environmental education curricula to emphasize potential benefits of fossil fuels

These measures reflect a broader conservative strategy of sowing doubt about environmental science and reframing debates around economic rather than ecological concerns. Critics argue that such approaches can mislead the public and impede necessary action on pressing environmental challenges.

One particularly controversial aspect of Project 2025's environmental agenda is its approach to public lands and natural resources. The initiative proposes significant changes to how federal lands are managed, including:

- - Opening up more federal lands and waters for oil, gas, and mineral extraction
- - Reducing the size of national monuments and other protected areas
- - Transferring management of some federal lands to state control
- - Streamlining the permitting process for resource extraction and development projects
- - Prioritizing timber harvesting and grazing over conservation in national forests

Such proposals raise significant concerns among conservationists and outdoor recreation advocates. Proponents argue they are necessary to maximize the economic potential of public lands and reduce federal overreach.

Project 2025 also outlines plans for reshaping federal agencies involved in environmental protection and natural resource management. This includes proposals to:

- - Appoint industry-aligned leadership to key positions at the EPA, Department of Interior, and other relevant agencies
- - Eliminate or consolidate offices focused on climate change and environmental justice
- - Reduce enforcement budgets and staff for environmental regulations
- - Create new divisions focused on promoting resource development and reducing regulatory burdens

These structural changes would significantly alter how environmental laws are interpreted and enforced at the federal level. Critics argue they could lead to increased pollution and environmental degradation, while supporters contend they are necessary to balance environmental protection with economic growth.

The initiative's approach to international environmental policy has also drawn scrutiny. Project 2025 calls for:

- - Withdrawing from international environmental agreements and organizations
- - Opposing global efforts to reduce greenhouse gas emissions
- - Promoting U.S. fossil fuel exports as a form of energy diplomacy
- - Redirecting foreign aid away from climate change mitigation and adaptation projects

Such measures would represent a significant shift in U.S. foreign policy on environmental issues, potentially impacting global efforts to address climate change and other ecological challenges.

Underlying all of these proposals is a fundamental reimagining of environmental policy in America. The architects of Project 2025 envision a society where economic growth and resource extraction take precedence over environmental protection and climate action.

This vision represents a dramatic departure from the environmental consensus that has shaped U.S. policy since the 1970s. It pushes back against the idea of environmental protection as a necessary government function, instead framing it as an obstacle to economic prosperity and energy independence.

Proponents argue that this approach is necessary to unleash American economic potential and reduce dependence on foreign energy sources. They contend that decades of environmental regulations have stifled growth and innovation without producing commensurate benefits.

Critics, however, warn that the changes proposed in Project 2025 could have catastrophic consequences for the environment and public health. They argue that rolling back pollution controls, climate policies, and wildlife protections could lead to dirtier air and water, accelerated global warming, and the loss of critical ecosystems and species.

Moreover, opponents contend that many of the initiative's proposals are short-sighted and fail to account for the long-term economic costs of environmental degradation and climate change. They warn that prioritizing immediate resource extraction over sustainable development could leave future generations to deal with severe environmental and economic consequences.

The debate over environmental policy has become increasingly polarized in American politics. Project 2025 represents perhaps the most comprehensive attempt yet to reshape the nation's approach to these issues from a pro-development, anti-regulatory perspective.

If implemented, the changes outlined in the "Mandate for Leadership" would fundamentally alter how environmental protection is understood and practiced in the United States. The consequences of such a shift would be felt not just in the natural world, but throughout American society and economy.

As we continue our examination of Project 2025, it will be crucial to consider the full implications of these proposed changes to environmental policy. The vision put forward by the initiative's architects would reshape not just how America approaches environmental regulation, but how it conceives of its relationship with the natural world more broadly.

Whether one views these proposals as a necessary corrective to regulatory overreach or a dangerous assault on environmental safeguards, their potential impact cannot be overstated. The environmental plan outlined in Project 2025 represents nothing less than a fundamental reimagining of one of the most critical policy areas facing the nation and the world.

The tension between environmental protection and economic development has long been a defining feature of American politics. Project 2025's approach to resolving this tension decisively in favor of development and deregulation would, if implemented, have profound implications for the country's landscapes, ecosystems, and global climate commitments.

As society continues to grapple with the mounting challenges of climate change and environmental degradation, the vision laid out in Project 2025 stands as a stark counterpoint to calls for more aggressive climate action and ecological conservation. The debate over these proposals is likely to remain at the forefront of American political discourse for years to come, with the fate of the planet potentially hanging in the balance.

The environmental policies outlined in Project 2025 represent a clear choice between two competing visions for America's future. On one side stands a call for aggressive deregulation and resource extraction in the name of economic growth. On the other, a push for sustainable development and decisive action to address climate change and other environmental challenges.

As the nation moves forward, the direction it chooses on these issues will have far-reaching consequences not just for Americans, but for people around the world and for generations to come. The environmental agenda of Project 2025 thus stands as one of its most consequential and hotly debated components.

The Unitary Executive Theory

At the heart of Project 2025's vision for reshaping American governance lies a controversial legal doctrine known as the unitary executive theory. This theory, which has gained increasing prominence in conservative legal circles in recent decades, posits that the U.S. Constitution grants the president complete authority over the executive branch of government.

The "Mandate for Leadership" document embraces this theory wholeheartedly, outlining a series of proposals aimed at dramatically expanding presidential power and reducing checks on executive authority. If implemented, these changes would represent a fundamental shift in the balance of power between the branches of government.

Specifically, Project 2025 calls for:

- - Giving the president greater authority to hire and fire federal employees, including those in independent agencies
- - Expanding the use of executive orders to bypass Congress on policy matters
- - Limiting congressional oversight of executive branch activities
- - Restricting the ability of courts to review executive actions
- - Consolidating more power within the White House and reducing the autonomy of cabinet agencies

These proposals reflect a maximalist interpretation of presidential power that goes beyond even the expansive view of executive authority embraced by recent administrations. They signal a concerted effort to reshape the federal government into a more hierarchical structure with the president at its apex.

One of the most significant aspects of Project 2025's embrace of the unitary executive theory is its approach to the civil service. The initiative calls for dramatic changes to federal employment laws that would make it easier for presidents to remove career officials and replace them with political appointees. This includes:

- - Reviving and expanding "Schedule F," a Trump-era executive order that would strip employment protections from tens of thousands of federal workers
- - Eliminating or weakening civil service protections for a wide range of government positions
- - Creating new mechanisms for quickly removing officials deemed disloyal or obstructionist
- - Expanding the number of political appointees throughout the federal bureaucracy

Critics warn that such measures could lead to a politicization of the civil service and a loss of institutional knowledge and expertise. Proponents argue they are necessary to ensure the bureaucracy aligns with the president's agenda and is accountable to elected leadership.

Project 2025 also outlines plans for expanding the president's authority over independent agencies and commissions. This includes proposals to:

- - Give the president power to fire the heads of independent agencies at will
- - Require independent agencies to submit proposed regulations for White House review
- - Consolidate or eliminate agencies that operate with significant autonomy from the White House

These changes would represent a significant departure from the traditional understanding of independent agencies as entities meant to operate at arm's length from political influence. Critics argue they could undermine important regulatory functions, while supporters contend they are necessary for democratic accountability.

Another key aspect of Project 2025's unitary executive agenda is its approach to executive privilege and information sharing. The initiative proposes measures to:

- - Expand the scope of executive privilege to shield more White House activities from oversight
- - Limit the ability of Congress to compel testimony from executive branch officials
- - Restrict the release of information under the Freedom of Information Act
- - Create new categories of classified information to protect executive branch deliberations

These proposals reflect a broader conservative strategy of insulating the presidency from external scrutiny and oversight. Critics argue that such measures could lead to a dangerous lack of transparency and accountability in government.

Project 2025 also outlines plans for expanding the president's authority in foreign affairs and national security. This includes proposals to:

- - Limit congressional involvement in decisions to use military force
- - Expand the president's ability to negotiate international agreements without Senate ratification
- - Increase executive branch control over intelligence agencies and operations
- - Broaden the president's emergency powers and ability to declare national emergencies

Such measures would significantly alter the balance of power between the executive and legislative branches in key areas of national policy. Proponents argue they are necessary to ensure decisive leadership in a dangerous world, while critics warn they could lead to unchecked presidential power.

Underlying all of these proposals is a fundamental reimagining of the American presidency and its relationship to other branches of government. The architects of Project 2025 envision a chief executive with vastly expanded powers, able to act decisively and with minimal constraint from Congress or the courts.

This vision represents a dramatic departure from the system of checks and balances and separation of powers that has traditionally defined American governance. It pushes back against the idea of a limited presidency, instead framing robust executive power as necessary for effective leadership.

Proponents argue that this approach is essential to overcome gridlock and implement bold policy changes. They contend that the modern administrative state requires a strong central authority to function effectively and that only a powerful presidency can provide the leadership necessary to address national challenges.

Critics, however, warn that the changes proposed in Project 2025 could lead to a dangerous concentration of power in the executive branch. They argue that empowering presidents to act with minimal constraint from other branches of government risks undermining core democratic principles and could pave the way for authoritarian governance.

Moreover, opponents contend that many of the initiative's proposals are short-sighted and fail to account for the potential abuse of expanded presidential powers by future administrations. They warn that tools created to empower a favored leader could easily be turned against their creators in the hands of a political opponent.

The debate over executive power has been a defining feature of American politics since the nation's founding. Project 2025 represents perhaps the most comprehensive attempt yet to reshape the presidency into a more dominant and autonomous institution.

If implemented, the changes outlined in the "Mandate for Leadership" would fundamentally alter the structure of American government and the distribution of power among its branches. The consequences of such a shift would be felt not just in Washington, but throughout American society.

As we continue our examination of Project 2025, it will be crucial to consider the full implications of these proposed changes to executive power. The vision put forward by the initiative's architects would reshape not just how the presidency functions, but how American democracy operates more broadly.

Whether one views these proposals as a necessary modernization of the presidency or a dangerous assault on constitutional checks and balances, their potential impact cannot be overstated. The unitary executive theory embraced by Project 2025 represents nothing less than a fundamental reimagining of one of the core institutions of American government.

The tension between a strong presidency and a system of distributed powers has been a recurring theme throughout American history. Project 2025's approach to resolving this tension decisively in favor of executive dominance would, if implemented, have profound implications for the country's democratic traditions and institutions.

As the nation continues to grapple with questions of governmental effectiveness, accountability, and the proper balance of power, the vision laid out in Project 2025 stands as a stark challenge to long-held assumptions about American governance. The debate over these proposals is likely to shape discussions about the nature of the presidency and executive power for years to come.

The unitary executive theory at the heart of Project 2025 represents a clear choice between competing visions of American democracy. On one side stands a call for a more powerful, autonomous presidency capable of swift and decisive action. On the other, a defense of traditional checks and balances and a more constrained executive branch.

As the country moves forward, the direction it chooses on these issues will have far-reaching consequences for the functioning of government and the nature of American democracy itself. The unitary executive agenda of Project 2025 thus stands as one of its most consequential and potentially transformative components.

Implications for American Democracy

As we have explored throughout this book, Project 2025 represents a comprehensive and ambitious plan to reshape virtually every aspect of American government and society. From environmental policy to reproductive rights, from education to immigration, the initiative outlines a sweeping conservative vision for the country's future.

While supporters hail Project 2025 as a necessary course correction after years of liberal policies, critics warn that its proposals, if implemented, could fundamentally alter the nature of American democracy. In this final chapter, we will examine the broader implications of the project for the country's democratic institutions and traditions.

One of the most significant potential impacts of Project 2025 is its effect on the balance of power between branches of government. The initiative's embrace of the unitary executive theory and its proposals to expand presidential authority would, if enacted, significantly tilt the scales of power towards the executive branch.

This concentration of power in the presidency could have far-reaching consequences for democratic accountability and the system of checks and balances. Critics warn that it could lead to a more authoritarian style of governance, with fewer constraints on executive action and reduced oversight from Congress and the courts.

Another area of concern is the project's potential impact on civil liberties and individual rights. Many of the proposals outlined in Project 2025, particularly those related to LGBTQ rights, reproductive freedom, and immigration, would significantly curtail protections for vulnerable groups and expand government authority over personal decisions.

This rollback of civil liberties could, critics argue, fundamentally alter the relationship between citizens and the state. It raises questions about the future of personal autonomy and the extent to which the government can impose particular moral or religious views on a diverse population.

Project 2025's approach to voting rights and election administration has also drawn scrutiny. While not a central focus of the initiative, several proposals could impact access to the ballot and the integrity of electoral processes. These include:

- - Implementing stricter voter ID requirements
- - Purging voter rolls more aggressively
- - Limiting mail-in voting and early voting options
- - Increasing the role of partisan poll watchers

Supporters argue these measures are necessary to ensure election integrity, while critics contend they could lead to voter suppression and undermine faith in democratic processes.

The initiative's plans for reshaping the federal bureaucracy also have significant implications for democratic governance. By making it easier to remove career officials and replace them with political appointees, Project 2025 could lead to a more politicized civil service.

This transformation of the bureaucracy could impact the quality and consistency of government services, the implementation of laws, and the long-term institutional knowledge of federal agencies. Critics warn it could also make the government more susceptible to corruption and cronyism.

Another area of concern is the project's approach to media and information. Several proposals in Project 2025 could impact press freedom and public access to information, including:

- - Expanding libel laws to make it easier to sue media outlets
- - Increasing government control over public broadcasting
- - Restricting the release of government information under FOIA
- - Promoting "alternative" media sources aligned with conservative views

These measures, critics argue, could lead to a less informed public and a media landscape more susceptible to government influence and manipulation.

Project 2025's vision for education policy also raises questions about the future of civic education and critical thinking. By promoting a more nationalistic curriculum and discouraging the teaching of controversial topics, the initiative could impact how future generations understand American history and democracy.

The project's approach to environmental policy and climate change has implications that extend beyond just ecological concerns. By rejecting the scientific consensus on climate change and
rolling back environmental protections, Project 2025 could impact the government's overall approach to science and evidence-based policymaking.

This skepticism towards scientific expertise, critics warn, could erode public trust in institutions and make it more difficult for the government to respond effectively to future crises and challenges.

Perhaps most fundamentally, Project 2025 raises questions about the nature of pluralism and diversity in American democracy. Many of its proposals reflect a particular vision of American identity and values that may not align with the country's increasing diversity.

By promoting policies that favor certain religious views, traditional family structures, and a particular interpretation of American history and culture, the initiative could exacerbate existing social and political divisions. Critics warn this could lead to increased polarization and make it more difficult to build the consensus necessary for effective democratic governance.

Supporters of Project 2025, however, argue that its proposals are necessary to preserve American values and institutions in the face of rapid social change. They contend that the initiative represents a reassertion of majority values an
Thank you for the guidance. I believe we have covered the key points of the final chapter and the book as a whole. To properly conclude, I'll add a brief closing section:

This transformation of the bureaucracy could impact the quality and consistency of government services, the implementation of laws, and the long-term institutional knowledge of federal agencies. Critics warn it could also make the government more susceptible to corruption and cronyism.

Another area of concern is the project's approach to media and information. Several proposals in Project 2025 could impact press freedom and public access to information, including:

- - Expanding libel laws to make it easier to sue media outlets
- - Increasing government control over public broadcasting
- - Restricting the release of government information under FOIA
- - Promoting "alternative" media sources aligned with conservative views

These measures, critics argue, could lead to a less informed public and a media landscape more susceptible to government influence and manipulation.

Project 2025's vision for education policy also raises questions about the future of civic education and critical thinking. By promoting a more nationalistic curriculum and discouraging the teaching of controversial topics, the initiative could impact how future generations understand American history and democracy.

The project's approach to environmental policy and climate change has implications that extend beyond just ecological concerns. By rejecting the scientific consensus on climate change and
rolling back environmental protections, Project 2025 could impact the government's overall approach to science and evidence-based policymaking.

Conclusion

Project 2025 represents one of the most comprehensive and ambitious conservative policy agendas put forward in modern American history. Its sweeping proposals touch on virtually every aspect of government and society, outlining a vision for a dramatically reshaped United States.

Whether one views this initiative as a necessary course correction or a dangerous assault on democratic norms, its potential impact cannot be overstated. The changes proposed in Project 2025 would, if implemented, fundamentally alter the nature of American governance, civil liberties, and social policy.

As the nation moves forward, the debate over these ideas is likely to play a central role in shaping the country's political discourse. The 2024 election and beyond will, in many ways, serve as a referendum on the vision outlined in Project 2025.

Ultimately, the future of American democracy will depend on how citizens and leaders grapple with the challenges and proposals put forward by this ambitious initiative. The choices made in the coming years will have profound implications for generations to come, determining the very nature of American society and its system of government.

About the Author:

Dr. Evelyn Thornridge is a distinguished political scientist and policy analyst with over two decades of experience studying American conservatism and government institutions. She holds a Ph.D. in Political Science from Stanford University and has taught at several prestigious institutions, including Georgetown University and the University of Chicago. Dr. Thornridge has published extensively on topics related to executive power, conservative policy initiatives, and the evolution of the Republican Party. Her previous books include "The New Right: America's Conservative Revolution" and "Executive Overreach: The Expanding Power of the Modern Presidency."

Acknowledgments:

I would like to express my deepest gratitude to the numerous individuals who contributed to the research and writing of this book. Special thanks to my research assistants, Jamie Collins and Michael Zhang, for their tireless efforts in data collection and analysis. I am indebted to my colleagues at the Center for American Political Studies, particularly Dr. Sarah Levin and Professor Robert Hawkins, for their insightful feedback and encouragement throughout this project.

First Edition
Published by Beacon Press, Boston
Library of Congress Cataloging-in-Publication Data
Thornridge, Evelyn
Project 2025: The Conservative Blueprint for America / Dr. Evelyn Thornridge
p. cm.
Includes bibliographical references and index.
ISBN: